ECHOES THAT STUTTER

ECHOES THAT STUTTER

Copyright © 2017 by Anirban Dam

Cover Photo Credit: Pius Lee (aka Travel Guy)

ISBN-13: 978-1543034479

ECHOES THAT STUTTER

Anirban Dam

Table of Contents

Chapter I

Windows in the Mist

MINOR UNCERTAIN POSSIBILITIES.

Like most nights, you lean against the window
(*a breeze caught between curtains and curfews*)
checking if the dogs are still awake,
wondering why the lamppost
across the street remains unfixed.

There is an urge to this farsightedness.

It is how the green in your eyes mimic
the grey in the air, and you point out tragedies
in the most trivial of details.

A freckle sliding down the shoulder,
a wrinkle unlearning to wilt.

At this point, the weather is merely a reference
to the unpredictable shifts in your thought
and much like the weather you leave
so much to chance.

Tonight, you are conviction clinging onto uncertainty.

Brittle to the bone,
chomping at the bit, aware
that the night will soon run its course.

But, it is not the sun that irks you
it's how the rays barge in unannounced —
a reminder that you left the window unlatched
in anticipation of nothing
or no one in particular.

BETWEEN NAUSEA AND NOSTALGIA.

Every static curtain is the wind
being deprived of its purpose

time and again it reminds us
how some windows aren't as welcoming as others.

This day unfolds like two palms
slowly unclasping from a prayer
prejudiced yet unaware of the
humdrum possibilities that await, but

sometimes it takes more than
a few routine chores to dissociate ourselves
from this unceasing vacancy which slowly enfolds us.
(*Meanwhile, the loaf of bread sitting unattended
on the counter begins to mould*)

How voiceless is this house
on a vapid Monday morning
when the lingering silence slowly
exfoliates the wrinkles in our tone.

How the reflection of a city
that has overstayed its welcome
slowly begins to hide behind the hems
of motionless drapes
(*perhaps, this is how a fist clenched with uncertainty
for too long reacts to a sudden breeze.*)

We are motes of dust, hovering
over deserted window sills; restless
and reluctant to settle down,
as if one day we will finally figure out the exact time
it takes for a moment to decompose into a memory
or a bread to turn stale.

EVANESCENT

watch —
   how a cloud crumbles,
then trickles down the window

   as if the sky is a canvas
and we're losing lustre as it rains

DOWNPOUR IN DECEMBER.

it's interesting how some songs
remind you of certain cities
and even though you haven't actually been there
you can still feel the cobblestone brush your feet
each time the chorus is about to start.

but, by the time this song ends, you'll be home
after another nauseous day
your hair tousled,
your rent overdue,
your fingers fatigued
from raking the vestiges of another passing season

soon, you garner the remnants
place it on your lap along with the frayed cardigan
(*a keepsake from a bygone passenger*)
but there isn't enough wool to patch the holes,
there isn't enough warmth to mend the wounds.

meanwhile,
the dogs wail,
the radio stutters,
the neighbours bicker,
the windows rattle,
and you watch this indignant city
pacified by a downpour
in December. the rain —
your lucky charm

WHEN THE RAIN REEKS OF HISTORY

[i]

Sometimes, I wonder how this city feels
when the sun melts on the horizon
and silhouettes of random couples
fade under the tapestry of unruly traffic
          restless to reach home, as if home is the place to be.

On the other end of the street there is you;
standing under a lamppost with your share of madness
carefully tucked in your bag
right next to the assignments
and that story
which you were never quite inclined to finish,
          mostly because you were still a bit sceptical
          about the conclusion.

So on your way back in the cab
          you examine the passing landscapes
and criticize modern architecture for its lack of affinity
          while the wind gets tangled in your hair
just enough to remind you how
some hearts function like doorknobs;

you have to twist them a little before
you could let someone in.

Originally published in *The Meadow, 2016*
Re-published in *In-flight Literary Magazine: Issue # 7*

[ii]

Don't ask the night
why it curls around like a question mark
right next to the urchin
who's sprawled like a hyphen on most days
        waiting for his latter half of existence
to combine with his current exigency of survival.

Because some poems,
they breed in gutters and bloom in graveyards.

Much like the mornings,
when you wake up like a creaking casket
with someone no longer breathing inside you

all the dead weight
curling around the strands of your hair

but you insist on leaving it open
because there's a cemetery in your clavicle
which you have to conceal.

[iii]

Tonight, the rain reeks of history
and each drop is re-enacting a sequence
        lost in time

ones which formed
a part of our curriculum
but we chose to discard
        due to the insignificance of their implication
        when compared to math or science.

So you no longer squint your eyes
or stretch your hand out
to feel a few drops of nostalgia
trickle down the creases of your palm
        because you can still feel the turbulence
        in your throat every time you say his name.

Sometimes, I wonder how you feel
when this city hides
behind the symmetry of a suburban household
as you close your curtains and the window
becomes a cage for everything trapped outside.

HOMAGE

the night sky is a eulogy gone wrong —
unknowingly, we've paid tribute
to many undeserving thoughts.

some days you highlight the repercussions of ageing
and on others, we analyse the fluidity of time.

our throats have grown into telescopes
now: they magnify our thoughts
way before the words form.

and at nights,
you stand by the window —
motionless, sifting through the tapestry
of industrial smoke like a mountain
that has ceased to grow. and I,

peer into the ocean of
unfamiliar faces on the road
hoping to measure these tiny spans of silence
with the rise and fall of their tidal feet.

EMERALD IN THE STORM

How easily did you seek comfort between tragedy and turmoil as if these eyes were born to grieve, not gleam.

"Endings are inevitable", you said, amid the indistinct murmur of unruly traffic and a Zeppelin song. Suddenly, the space between our shoulders widened to accommodate the awkward stillness. I swear if silence had a shape then it would be a triangle — so that people would chisel the frost off their tongues with its very edges every time they run out of things to say. But then again, it was these very moments when I could hear the uproar in your voice as if your sinews could no longer confine the skirmish inside the marrows and your eyes would light up like a beacon in a war zone. Maybe, that's why you always wear the night like armour, to shelter yourself from the ambush of streetlights because you know that someone, somewhere with a makeshift house still sleeps under a lamppost mistaking it for the moonlight and that somewhere, on the other side of the equator, is a sun, which still gets strangled by the horizon every single day. But these scars go deeper. Way deeper than the ligature marks on the sun. I know how your legs still tremble every time a wave kisses your feet — reminding you of dead lovers or how you can only rise to your feet in your sleep like a somnambulist who's been walking on eggshells for too long because in the end you are destined to break someday like most beautiful things are. But then again, you were born with enough grace in your bones to even make your slivers shine.

Chapter II

Beginning of the Sky

DISTANCE & DELIRIUM.

*"As if you could kill time without injuring eternity." - **Henry David Thoreau***

It was as if
we had finally learned to dismiss
the complexities of this seemingly futile world,
where cities bask in insipid reveries
stemming from numerous what-ifs
simmering inside every household
while another day drags its feet past our door.

But we are no longer trying to make sense of this quiet
that lingers between my pocket and your purse
every time our instincts breach each other's periphery.

And even though my hands tremble a little,
and even though your breath fumbles
past my beard like a lisp leaving us hesitant
like the night which is reticent and sweating nervously
but you insist on calling it rain for some reason

we stand there quietly with a fistful
of uncertainty between us;
watch each drop plummet like a refrain between
this distance and delirium, while time
sheds its skin and leaves us naked on the brink of eternity.

NOUMENON.

soon
after dusk
drops its shoulders
&
surrenders to the indifference
of a city
shipwrecked on the idea
that time never grows old

you rest your head
on my chest
&
tell me how you don't feel good
(*for no apparent reason*)

I silently stroke your hair
&
watch eternity age
in the corner of your lips.

UNVEILED

I wake —
to the landscape
  of her freckled back

a bruise peeking
over her neck

there is an unfathomable intimacy
between vision and sight.

MONOTONY OF SWOLLEN CLOUDS.

There is something about the wind
which strays into a cemetery
every night in search of a home,
the same way we wake up
to the monotony of swollen clouds
every morning,
wondering if
the air still reeks of myths
which clawed their way
into our reticent conversations.

I like the way
you obsess about little details.
How the spoons should be on the right
or how the bed sheet tag
should be on the lower left
and I'm not afraid to admit
that I might fuck this up
multiple times before I finally realize
that your left is my right,
but I am willing to try
one more time
so I could show you
how sides don't matter when
we're lying next to each other
like two lumps of cold
on a Christmas morning
with so much warmth
in our breaths that the mere thought
of touching each other's face
can melt all the ice
on our tongue.

There is something about the moon
that gets tangled in the curtains
in search of a mason jar
the same way gods plummet into my lap
when I unbraid your hair
and you tease me for being too gentle.

DAWN

how
    the light
strokes her skin
every morning

as if the sun
        kneels
on her window
in search of absolution

UNTITLED # 55

like most days,
there's too much stillness lurking
beneath these dialogues, but I am finally
learning to fathom each pause,
decipher each wrinkle in your tone,
count every freckle on your breath but
this rigidity under my tongue
still manages to stifle me at times.

yet your name echoes between
a voice and a verb like an action
unaware of its consequence. maybe,
there's a reason why your words keep missing
the mark by a split second,
maybe there's a reason why my
hindsight keeps hiding in my back pocket
right next to the spare change

perhaps there's adequate menace
in our mouths to paint the night
into something so perverse that
our limbs might tremble at the very thought of dawn

 Originally published in *In-flight Literary Magazine: Issue # 8*

Chapter III

Absent Moons

❖ A day on Mercury is two Mercurian years long i.e. approximately 58.65 earth days.
❖ Daylilies usually have a lifespan of 24 hours

MERCURY.

Back when dinosaurs
roamed the earth each
year consisted of 370 days.
Apparently, time is ageing.
You can feel the fatigue in
its arms every time it's 3.45 or 9.15.
The moon is becoming heavier
each day, its gravity is
acting as a drag and hence
days are getting longer
by 1.7 millisecond per century.

At this rate,
soon there will be grey in our hair
and grief in our bones.
We will feel it in our knees every
time it rains and I
am certain that even after
all these years I
still wouldn't know how
to fold bed sheets the *right way*
or make a decent bowl of soup
every time you catch a cold.
But all you can think of is
your garden.

Time is a fractal.

We are patterns repeating
ourselves day in day out.

I press my palm over your bellybutton
(*time moves relatively slower
when you're closer to the centre of the earth*)

One day on Mercury is two years long, I say.
You look out through the window and
wonder what it would be like to
watch the daylilies bloom and wither
58.65 times every day.

SILENCE IS AN ANAGRAM

[i]

on days when
we are no longer willing
        to fight the urge of acceptance
        and the dogs across the street
are unresponsive
to cars and walking cadavers

I stand on the window juggling our
predictable conversations
        camouflaged by the backdrop
        of insipid households
which are pacified in the glare of
10 p.m. news
or reality shows

and my reality
        stands under a streetlight tonight

in a world which hangs so heavy
and hollow like the countless
wombs laden with
the prospect of
creation

                but
        we breathed so many elegies
        down each other's neck
        our bodies look like
        obituaries now,
        when splayed on a bed sheet
        our pillows —
        ossify into
        tombstones

            Originally published in *The Meadow, 2016*

[ii]

     Sunday breeze
     rattles the wind chime
and you are brewing a maelstrom in your cup

you once said
silence is an anagram —
it can be rearranged in many ways
without making a sound

so we sleep quietly on weekends

     mourning the things we said,
     detesting the things we didn't

[iii]

this afternoon is clumsy
it holds us like your flimsy gown
which keeps slipping off your shoulders frequently

there's too much slack on our skin.

[iv]

on weekdays
you inspect ideologies
of heartbreaks and hedonism

bending hypotheticals
to fit our reality
(you are only as decadent as your insecurities)

but I have shed
my symmetry long ago
when the sky relinquished its shape

so pull your dusk
out of my hair
I am done playing
the horizon for everything
receding into the distance.

CROP CIRCLES.

It's quite an intriguing phenomenon, you say.
Almost convinced that its occurrence is purely natural.
For once, you're leaning towards insight
as opposed to evidence.

Sometimes, their shapes and structures are suggestive
of some cyclonic wind reaction —
much like our house
by the end of each month.

The alignment of your clothes
depicting the turbulence in your thoughts,
the symmetry of my beard
accentuating the indifference in my tone.
(*with hindsight, behaviour evolves into predictable patterns*.)

*Or maybe they're just hoaxes
or geometric pranks*, you say.
Your clavicle pushing up against my chin,
my fingers orbiting your navel.

Probability works best when the variables
are unknown, not estranged.

So much remains unresolved
between your analysis of instinct
and my interpretation of fact.

SILHOUETTES

And finally,
when the night curls up under
the blanket and you are no longer
sifting dreams from dust, I stand
over the window holding the skyline
like a forgotten silhouette and
we watch this city burn
in the creases on our palms.
Meanwhile, the stars are learning to recover
from daylight and the space between us
keeps shifting like the ebb and flow
till we become progressions;
lost between the tunes of melody and malice.
So leave your hair open and the door unlocked,
let the moon hide behind your curls,
tonight we speak nothing but silence
in our native tongues.

HOLLOW

there is
    an insurmountable vacancy
coiled inside her
carefully suppressed
    beneath her ribs.

some nights you can hear
her breathe like a stuttering flute

SHE HARBOURS HURRICANES IN HER HEART

[i]

she skins the sun with bare hands
to drape herself in a radiance bright enough
to hide between headlights and rear-view mirrors

in a city where walls are wounded
and graffiti bled after two a.m. past
street fights.

[ii]

there are memories
on her shoulders, slouching
like a leper who knows
the pain of numbness
while her spine
stretches out like a harpoon

long enough to keep her from
tossing her head back
yet short enough
to keep her from sitting straight

so she walks around
with yesterdays tucked between her legs
and letters stuck between
her teeth as if she chewed
silence with her mouth open

but nostalgia has a way
of cluster fucking people
till they become reminders
stuck between reveries and recaps.

[iii]

there are days,
when she fucks strangers behind cemeteries
so, death would know
the sound when she finally came
in a casket,
or a basket

with wreathes on her chest and
wrath in her hair
seeking reprieve from a world
where god plays the widow
so, the sky would dress in black
while the day
sheds its dignity
like a righteous whore.

but then,
there are days when her heart
pounds like a loose cannon
and you could hear
the war cry of her soul
in every beat

as she dances
under meadows and moonlights
like a motion stuck between
release and retreat
while oceans parch inside her mouth
to quench the thirst
of endless possibilities
and she shines
in a way
unfamiliar to stars.

PRISM

watch —
   the air distort
her face along
   with the moon
  with each passing ripple

some reflections lack
depth and disposition

NOTES FROM AN OBSCURE PLANET.

On this planet, there are gods who worship men for their might and whisper their names sincerely every night. There is a *Van Gogh* in every home right next to *Gandhi*, but in this version, *Gandhi* is not a warrior. In fact, he's a writer, who wears baggy jeans and ends up in bar fights on most nights because he believes that freedom isn't freedom unless every god has the right to call a certain man a dick, even though some might consider it profane. He uses the word fuck and its variants very frequently in his writings and as for Van Gogh — he secretly paints underpasses and boarded up windows with aerosol cans at night under an assumed identity, *Banksy*.

On this planet, the memory of a kiss is erased as soon as the tiny little hairs on the back on your neck settle down, so that you can relive every single kiss with a perfect newness as if it was your first. So, for the teens, every kiss is followed by a horror movie to sustain the goose bumps and as for the adults — they rediscover each other several times every night. 71% of this planet is occupied by sky and oceans are an endless entity stretching above your head. Hence, each day begins at sun set and we fall in bed when the sun rises and it's phenomenal how the rain rises from under your feet and leaves you weak in the knees. There are old women who dig up lightning from the skies and preserve them in mason jars only to sell them as wind chimes during a thunderstorm and there are florists sell bouquets of constellation because no one here wishes on a falling star. People on this planet sweat when they are sad but sweatshirts and sweatpants will not have been invented in the next 200 years. Up here, time is a relative concept, so everyone falls in love at their own pace and love is inversely proportional to space; that is to say that everyone falls apart in closer proximities. Over here, flowers have overgrown beards and a mimosa will open up when you touch it, only when you've finally found closure. On this planet, *fuck* is a polite word.

Chapter IV

Remains to be seen.

EXPLAINING GRIEF TO MY DAUGHTER.

Dear __________,

There will come a day when you'll tie your shoes with the strands of my hair to keep your feet from shivering each time you hear a siren or see an ambulance passing by. But believe me, somehow your limbs will still keep falling like timber on concrete, your kneecaps will flip inside out like suction cups and your eyelids will start fluttering like staplers; pinning every single thought of me with the body bags under your eyes. But don't stop, keep blinking… they'll run out of pins someday. *I will no longer be a pinprick on your skin when that happens.*

Sometimes, it will take more than just a few self-help books to accept the fact that absence is not a state of mind when your eyes deliberately start missing out on little details, objects and gradually, persons till you realize that the shadows on your wall will only stretch out as far as your imagination. *Leave the lights on and close your eyes. I'll be watching over you while you sleep.*

Some days, you'll trip over your own feet while your fist will still be clenched with the fear of uncertainty. It's not the physical pain nor the fear of humiliation that will ache, but it will be that very moment when you look down to tie your shoelace and realize that you've been walking barefoot all along. That's when the coat on your shoulder will turn into a straitjacket, tight enough to restrain your tears yet soft enough to make you feel secure. *Remember my embrace.*

Soon, you will feel paradigms shifting under your breastplates and your insides will feel like gravels; spinning and swivelling like fragments in a kaleidoscope but by then you would've already learned to wear god like a scarf to conceal the confessions on your chest like a devout atheist. Yet the crucifix between your breasts will keep piercing your flesh deeper and deeper every single day till the edges of your ribs start pricking your heart; just enough to puncture your soul with every single heartbeat. Reach out for me, whisper my name. I'll fold you in my arms and hold you tight till the sounds of your crumbling insides become the lullabies for your nightmares.

Some nights, those unsaid words will fasten your ankle like an anchor drowning you in this static pool of silence. On such nights, remember that your cheeks have been brushed by hands which have carved roadways between mountains and your skin has been stitched with the very thread which keeps the equator from falling right above your head — don't you ever fall apart. Remember that anxiety is not your inheritance, suicide is not hereditary, depression is not a lifestyle and that the roots of your foundation are strong enough to keep you grounded to the core even when the earth beneath your feet is shifting. *Breathe a little. Water the plants daily.*

And finally, there will come a day when you will have to draw a
tunnel on your wall and gather enough courage to punch your fist on
it 'till to see the light at the end and your throat will be filled with
skid marks from words which crashed and burned on your tongue.
But keep smiling. Don't let gravity pull down the corners of your
lips because one day the sky will split at the seams, the clouds will
fall like confetti on your bed and you'll wake up with poetry tangled
in your hair. It won't hurt to open the blinds anymore.

I remain,
Dad.

P.S.: One day I will find the right words, and they will be simple

TWO TABLESPOONS ANALOGY AND A PINCH OF SALT.

two decades and a handful of years later
you realized that even two people
wanting the exact same thing, when placed
in a same room can feel lonely together.

my mother always kept the spices on the top shelf
along with the pickles and the jar of salt
(but never sugar nor honey.
she'd always keep them on the bottom shelf)
and due to her tall and slender build it was
always within her grasp.

she'd say that everyone should always
have something sweet within their reach
and that no one should have to struggle for it.
but that is how it is with the most of us —
we struggle to seek the things we
need the most, and by the time we acquire it
we no longer possess the struggle to justify what we need.

two people in the same room
are struggling to reach the salt.

you watch their fingers flutter for a while
before they finally give up and fall still
like dandelions —

swaying,
stationery,
slowly disintegrating beneath a motherless roof.

this is how grief appears to the naked eye
when within striking distance.

DENSITY

another leaf withers —
    lands on my shoulder
    and suddenly i
am reminded of you.

        you weigh half a cloud
and a fistful of uncertainty.

CLOUD SHAPED CASKETS.

The hostile wind piercing the dense leaves breaks
another branch and dismantles a nest
in the process. Three eggs tumble out
of the nest.

The first one splatters instantly,
the second one is somewhere between
splinter and survival but the third one
has only begun to crack.
Flock of scavengers gather around
and wait for the wind to settle,
the mother is unable to locate her cradle.

(*It is moments like these when one fully fathoms
the nuance between crisis and calamity*)

I once asked you why
cemeteries are so quiet at night
and that if I dug a little deeper would I be able to see
how they really look like on the inside?

It's because when people die
they turn into stars, you said
and silently gazed at the sky as if it was
the vast uninterrupted surface of a boneyard
and clouds were asymmetrical caskets
with really tight but transparent lids.

The third egg hatched a little more.

UNTITLED # 48

She said, she'd breakdown and cry till her hands were steady enough to hold my ashes and watch them drift away between her fingers till I became a part of something larger than life. That way, she would feel my presence every time the waves kissed her feet. It was amazing how simple her thoughts were until today, when I realized the courage it takes to keep a steady hand — knowing how the weight of twenty years would scatter away that very moment I split these fingers and I stood there wondering how she said it all with a smile on her face.

IN PROPORTION TO DEATHS DIALECT.

There are time zones shifting in my mouth
as I wake up to this day holding perspective
like my mother's indecisiveness
between fish and poultry

but not everything can be fathomed in
calories and proteins.

There are windows losing their vision,
widows losing their virginity,
words shedding their tenses
and I am standing under streetlights

like a Petri dish
with enough agar on my skin
to make the light bounce off my skull
at an angle between incidence and inception

hoping that the sky is fertile enough
to be impregnated with a glint of light
so it gives birth to another day

because I have seen
a thousand things darker than the night.

I've seen the light
dwindle on a grave half my size
and one fourth my age,
the shadow of a hooker
slowly lose its identity.

So daylight, stretch your arms
embrace this city with your fingertips
and hold it against your beating chest.

Hear the turbulence of households
rattling in their wind chimes,
the rumble of relationships between dirty dishes,
feel the tremors of small talks
collapsing on dinner tables
tickle your heart every day
when they're passing the salt.

There are time zones
shifting inside my mouth
like a kaleidoscope
and my breath smells like
forgotten yesterdays with a
hint of yogurt.

MY WORDS WERE ALL I COULD OFFER

I still
remember that night
when the boughs started breaking
like promises and you slept
on a pile
of dried up leaves
waiting to be raked
by the uncertainty of
another passing season.

Now I didn't know much
about mowing a lawn
but I learned that only grass
had a kind of blade
which didn't make you bleed
and you said,
it's been so long that
I've forgotten how spring feels like.

So, I started slipping words
in the vase you kept on your nightstand
hoping they'd bloom into poems one day
from all the dew dripping
down your eyelash
all those times
you'd stand across the looking glass
wondering how you would look like
if you tied your hair in a bun,
but you had none.

spring never came.

Soon, days transpired into nights,
the nights became nuances
amidst dawn and dusk
leaving you confused
between the darkness
that had just arrived and
the light which had caught rust

and radiation
became the remedy
for everything malignant
but your lips were the only thing
which never metastasized
into smiles,
and I know how you loved to smile.

You'd smile every time it rained.

You'd say,
that rain is the sky's way of holding on
to the earth despite the distance
and that droplets were liquid strings
connected to tin cans on both ends
and that's how gods and mortals make amends.
You see, nothing falls in vain.

So I wrote you a cloud
because pillows weren't soft enough
to bury your face
for all those rainy days
because your windows were slowly becoming
colour blind from all the grey
and now I know how curtains feel
when the sun pierces through their skin
kissing the foot of your bed
reminding you how every day is one day less.

 But I am no magician
to make you a cape
stitched from all the cure
for flying off is better
than fading away,

So I offer you my words
to alleviate the pain
take them,
take them
so I can write you a mountain
with letters coated in vertigo
so you would never dare to look down
when I frown or become hell bound
because I'm still learning
to hang bulls eye patches
on my blind spots,
to hide
your exit wounds.

THE SPACE BETWEEN SILENCE.

Never turn your back while exiting a temple,
it brings bad luck. Almost a decade later
these words have resurfaced again
(*mothers usually tend to show up unannounced*)

only this time you are willing to explore
the undertones in that statement.

Back then, your understanding of the word back
was constricted. A patch of skin evenly spread
between nape & tailbone, partially visible without a mirror.

You didn't know about organ systems —
the inversely proportional relationship between eyes & feet.

How each receding footstep shrinks a landscape
to fit your perspective.

The horizon gradually reduced to a hyphen, the skyline
compressed to resemble the cuts on your door key.

How fickle is this estrangement
which grows with each receding footstep, how uncertain
the distance which occupies this ever increasing space.

This is how grief operates.
It tricks you into turning your back

and instantly all this blur around you sharpens itself into focus,
every single strand of noise slowly evaporates.

All that is left behind is a sound
desperately trying to find its voice.

Silence couldn't possibly be more inarticulate.

Chapter V

Some Rooms Require Constant Repairs

1

Some days, you want to lease this room
to evenly redistribute this vague sense of vacancy
and on others, you chronologically rearrange
every single object
or simply scrape the dust
off every untouched surface
till there's nothing left to erase.

Even though March is unresponsive to
dry coughs and second hand comfort
there is yet a subtle tenderness
in the not so sterile air which clings onto your skin,
and somewhere between nausea and nostalgia
you press your ear against the glass window.

The fatigue in the wind
reveals a certain semblance
to the many conversations piled up on the window sill,
and silently you watch the skyline succumb to
a dusky silhouette.

But little did you know that
we would grow up into empty receptacles
that spend most of their rainy days
staring at the leaking roof.

And as for
this city and its calloused feet,
the streets and their clogged arteries,
the moon and its overpriced gleam,
the doors and their creaking spine,

everything grows a little wearier each day,
every room becomes less feral with time.

2

When the front door was finally
being replaced, you wondered how
fifteen years ago the movers managed
to fit the large Oakwood dining table through such
a small space. It was a small house
but adequate in every sense.

You'd always ask why the walls were
so rough or so unevenly plastered
or how come we didn't have any
photographs on them, only posters of gods and goddesses
(*strategically placed to conceal the cracks*)

It's because we're out of nails,
mother would reply. We were always
out of nails but never out of nurture.
And after fifteen years of repairs and reforms
you understood how doors depreciate.

How an entrance grows smaller each year
because no one is willing to open up,
and how you sure as hell cannot remove
the old Oakwood table in a single piece.

Now, when the carpenter's gone,
mother wipes the sawdust off the photo frames.
*We were never out of nails, it's just that
we never had perfect pictures back then,*
she said. You take a closer look
at the pictures —
realize how each wall
is smooth and meticulously plastered now.
How each heart is wearing a brace.

3

Outside, the photographs
in the hallway emit colour each Thursday
and maybe you will never look more insipid
than you do over here.

It's quite peculiar how so much
can remain unsaid in those tiny crevices
between nudging shoulders and despite
the conspicuous lingering silence,
those overdone domestic smiles get the benefit of doubt.
But you were never a good liar.
Wandering eyes, awkward smile, crooked lips as
if they were meant to conceal beneath them but it's
the gaps between your teeth that always gave you away.

As a child, you've moved a lot but
the fundamentals of a home remained the same.
The heavy furniture was always close
to the exit, the fancy cutlery never made it out
of the bubble wraps, the walls were always bleached,
and doors were just a metaphor for everything
closing behind your back.

But eventually, after a certain point, you stopped
growing up in the houses you once occupied
and home started ageing in the gaps between your teeth.

Perhaps, that is when you finally made amends with
the squeaky hinges and came to terms with the
faces which had gradually learned to blend into
the blurry background with each passing Thursday.

4

This house wears a dialect —
the kind only you can comprehend.

Cobwebs are hieroglyphs
they only make sense on things gathering dust.

Outside, the gimpy table still struggles to find balance
its surface scored with your initials;
each carving less wobbly than the prior.
(*your A's are stable and symmetrical now*)

The floorboards have acclimatized to
biased footing, the cabinets

well within grasp.
Your toes have grown unfamiliar
to the urge of reaching out for something.

Some days you stand here like an outsider
unable to segregate
home from house,

and the window —
slides just enough
to reel in the sky one cloud at a time.

Chapter VI

Trinkets of Time.

UNTITLED # 46

Her eyes carried a certain weight like the sighs of hundred men who missed the last train to meet their wives. Yet, her eyelids would flutter like they could confine every fleeting moment in the corner of her eyes. She was made of metaphors, sinews stitched with similes and it was beautiful how she couldn't care less as she made snow angels on the ground even when her serrated heart would beat like a hacksaw chiselling every single marrow — the specks from her bones would drizzle like flakes on a summer night. She truly lived in the moments which made her feel alive even though her eyes carried a certain weight. The weight of uncertainty. The uncertainty of tomorrow.

WHEN THE CREASES ON YOUR SHIRT OUTNUMBER THE FURROWS ON YOUR FOREHEAD

[i]

    if you shave at night
before you go to bed, skip breakfast
and leave eight minutes early

there's a good chance
that you might not run into
    the persistent old woman who is determined to
hand you yesterday's newspaper
because she's too proud to accept your charity
without offering something in return.

for a brief moment, you might be relieved,
but soon you'll miss reading the horoscope
and mock astrology for yet another inaccurate prediction
of a day which was yet to unfold yesterday
but it's a vague coincidence that somehow
your shirt managed to match
the suggested "lucky colour" on most days
(except when it's red, yellow, green or pink)

    and despite your compulsive need
to fold the paper ergonomically to minimize the creases
there's something so reassuring about
a small turmeric stain on its edge
which tells you that she didn't sleep
with an empty stomach last night

[ii]

there is a nuance between news and nuisance,
one which can't be found in the fine prints of politics
            and despite your apolitical stance
you are forced to become a leftist on most days
because the train is packed and your right hand
        is glued to the handle over your head.
amid all the indistinct chatter
you are trying to complete a half solved crossword
        but you were always terrible at crosswords
        just like you're terrible with names

        but you're always good with faces
because each face renders a certain quirkiness
which a name can never dispense —

        maybe that's why you never asked
that old lady her name
but you remember the exact look on her face
        every time she goes through the obituary section,

    the way she shakes her head and poses a crooked smile
  when she tells you that even something like death
has such a short lifespan in a newspaper
  or when she asks you whether they'll publish her photo
    when she dies and write a few fancy words for her

but you don't have the heart to tell her that
it's rather expensive and tricky
to grieve for someone
in a 4" x 2" grave
given the limited word count

so you shave at night before you sleep,
skip your breakfast and spend the next eight minutes
        trying to rewrite the ending of this poem
        which has held its breath for way too long

because sometimes tomorrow is just yesterday in a wrinkled shirt

CLOUD

she writes
    of rain and rancour
folds it carefully
and holds it
        against her bosom
when she sleeps.

there is a cloud
    inside her chest
which hasn't poured in years.

NICOTINE AND NIETZSCHE AT 180 BPMS.

there are days when you hold the sky by its edges
to fathom the vastness of infinity between
your arms, only to realize that you're concave
and confined within a peripheral vision of reality.
myopia?

so you breathe —
a little dust,
a little dismay,
and just enough disappointment
to coat your lungs with asbestos
and cognitive dissonance
then stare out the window and
watch street lights getting mugged,
shadows getting groped
and you wonder how the city sustains itself
with each passing day, feeling smug.

then, there are days when you see
a man across the street leisurely scratching his balls.
you quickly criticize and condemn the theories
of evolution while the complacency
in your coffee turns tepid.

we are minute, like the grains in an hourglass
shifting,
        drifting incessantly;
a perennial cycle
so you assign weekends for building castles
with sands of time on tide-less shores
till you drown in the streams of
your very own consciousness

and finally, there's that day when you trade
your hard earned epiphany for another box
of Marlboro knowing how there's a revelation
in every cigarette you smoke and a resolution
in every smoke you exhale

while the clenched fist clogging your windpipe
opens up to catch the lumps
and moulds in your throat
which fall face first like the arrival of autumn.

soon you realize that there are too many
~~you's~~ I's in the poems
~~you write~~ I write
and concentricity turns into narcissism

but a man is merely the consequence of
his very thought, an echo resonating
in a vacuum called time till he is nothing
but a parallel of his own shadow, you say

then pluck another leaf out
of Nietzsche's book
to reaffirm and restore
your dwindling faith
in atheism and

move on to analyse
the possibility of space time singularity

WE WERE EPILOGUES LOOKING FOR CLOSURE.

I have seen you
leaning against the window
like a gentle breeze
caught between
curtains and curfews

gazing at this city
that sleeps with

its mouth open
like an empty ashtray
pointed towards the sky
hoping to catch a star
on its tongue

burning like a cigarette
between fingers of a god
who knows how
the rush of nicotine,
is the only thing that
keeps his windpipes from clogging.

*(we all have different reasons
to hold and catch our breath.)*

I know that
there's a typewriter
lodged somewhere
between your breasts
whose keys
batter your chest like
a broken bass drum
every time you swallow a word

but let's not become
those unwritten poems tonight,
which lost their essence
between fact and fiction

because our verses weren't
strong enough to lift
dreams and dilemmas
at the same time.

Let's not wear caution
like a Kevlar and become
vulnerable for a change

so that when the right words
come to strike us
we'd bleed into epitaphs
onto the tombstones
we've been carrying in our back pockets
because endings are inevitable

and we are merely
poorly scripted epilogues
looking for closure.

UNSENT CORRESPONDENCE.

June 6, 1980: it was raining

you enter
like a wet dream
soaked in certainty
that warmth served in cafes
are distilled and bastardized.

I slipped a poem in your purse

June 8, 1980: strings and tin cans

a quarter
clinks through the coin slot

I say two hells… three hellos…
and one fluently faltered Helen.

you chortled like a conspicuous inside joke

August 8, 1980: one night stands

> we stood like cathedrals
> built on a benefit of doubt
> that faith emerges from desire,
> not desperation.
>
> I left a prayer in your belly button.

August 10, 1980: you wait by the phone while your coffee turns cold

I found my poem
crinkled on the kerb

sold it for three quarters
and kept them by the payphone

if only I had known that
someone snatched your purse yesterday

WHEN A NAME RUSTS.

[i]

on days
when you have missed the last bus
and the train station is four and a half songs away

do you hail a cab or
do you take a walk
past that shady restaurant, you once liked
because its happy hours truly made you smile

      or do you take a detour
walk past the vendors who are busy gathering
the leftovers of another tedious evening
while their prodding eyes blink
      in unison with the broken lamppost over their heads

[ii]

      you wonder how a concept so vast
as life can be reduced to a mere act of survival

perhaps this is the closest you'll ever come
to watch the light erupt into a language
as fluent as the winter breeze
      reminding you of chapped lips and weary eyes
      and the dire need to keep them moist

because nostalgia is only as useful as an ambulance
when you're trying so hard not to let someone die inside you

[iii]

and it's strange how some nights are composed
from recaps or renditions and it's those exact nights
when you're vexed because there's a tune in your head
          which you can't quite figure

perhaps this is the closest you'll ever come
to watch a chorus collapse in the middle
          of the street while the song
scatters past the conversations of
deadbeat men uneager to meet their wives

so you lick your lips,
hail a cab,
lower the window and sink beneath
the commotion of this wakeful city
which slowly fills the back seat
because you know
how an echo tastes when a name
rusts in your throat.

RITUAL.

December is a liturgy —

everything that we once
held sacred is cremated
amid the leaves.

This fire is either a scum or a saint.

It devours parts of us
which is no longer required.

Every year,
we sit by the flame
hoping to rekindle
something which is now
a distant memory

and when the fumes settle

between us lingers
a handful of smoke and a half-hearted prayer.

LIMINALITY.

it is quite unnatural to watch a city
being consumed by its own vacancy in the middle of the night,
when every household is transitioning
                    from a sigh to a snore
and the hum of the refrigerator is trying to suppress
the sound of this restlessness which keeps tugging at your ribs.

        it's funny how you thought streets shrink
a little each day as we grow, and by the time
we're fully grown there will be neighbourhoods colonising
beneath our fingertips and that is when
we finally stop biting our nails

but sometimes childhood grows up way before
we learn to grow out of it.

you can be in conflict with yourself on most nights
even when you're sober
(when it comes to love or loss)
but eventually, absence is best explained
and understood in one's native tongue.
                    and tonight,
you are just a song away from relapse —
there is a certain impediment in your breath,
a certain muteness in your sight,
and you're somehow fighting off the urge
to bite your nails

        because you know that in the end,
we are all woven into this insurmountable silence
which surrounds us, yet you are unable
to rephrase this quiet into a common dialect.

it is quite unnatural to watch an echo
stutter in the middle of the night.

CONUNDRUM

The sun withdraws earlier than usual
undressing the clouds on its way out
(*the city is yet to reveal its true colours*)

From here, the street is a patchwork of bustling collars

he examines them like alphabets —
scurrying, unaware of their placement,
their gait seldom making sense.

In moments like these
the sky is a palindrome
and the smoke between his fingers
is a lingering static
yet to assume his shape.

Some days, dusk calibrates
the tint in his eyes, on others
he watches society disintegrate from the rooftop
(*a spectrum of possibilities happening all at once*)

it remains unclear how
sequence bridges the gap
between inference and instinct.

For now, he settles for a cursory resolve
and an abrupt ending.

ABOUT THE AUTHOR

Anirban is a twenty something parasite who thrives on guilt-free sarcasm and gluten-free poetry.